Family Members

Debbie Gallagher

Marshall Cavendish
Benchmark
New York

This edition first published in 2009 in the United States of America by Marshall Cavendish Benchmark.

Marshall Cavendish Benchmark
99 White Plains Road
Tarrytown, NY 10591
www.marshallcavendish.us

All Internet sites were available and accurate when sent to press.

First published in 2008 by
MACMILLAN EDUCATION AUSTRALIA PTY LTD
15–19 Claremont St, South Yarra 3141

Visit our Web site at www.macmillan.com.au or go directly to www.macmillanlibrary.com.au

Associated companies and representatives throughout the world.

Copyright © Debbie Gallagher 2008

Library of Congress Cataloging-in-Publication Data

Gallagher, Debbie, 1969-
    Family members / by Debbie Gallagher.
        p. cm. — (Families)
    Includes index.
    ISBN 978-0-7614-3139-8
    1. Family—Juvenile literature. 2. Genealogy—Juvenile literature. I. Title.
    HQ744.G37 2008
306.85—dc22

                                                    2008001670

Edited by Georgina Garner
Text and cover design by Christine Deering
Page layout by Raul Diche
Photo research by Brendan Gallagher

Printed in the United States

Acknowledgments

The author and the publisher are grateful to the following for permission to reproduce copyright material:

Front cover photograph: Family blowing bubbles together © Blend Stock Photos

Photos courtesy of: Big Cheese Photos, 14; Blend Stock Photos, 1, 10, 27; Corbis Royalty Free, 12; © Marilyna/Dreamstime.com, 28–29 (background); © Mcininch/Dreamstime.com, 15; © Pascalepics/Dreamstime.com, 11; The DW Stock Picture Library, 3, 8, 9, 18, 21, 25; © D.Ducouret/Fotolia, 19; © sonya etchison/Fotolia, 13; © Pascale Wowak/Fotolia, 23; Getty Images/Image Source, 6; Getty Images/Photodisc, 20; © North Georgia Media L.L.C./iStockphoto, 4; Phil Weymouth/Lonely Planet Images, 24; © 2734725246/Shutterstock, 7; © digitalskillet/Shutterstock, 5; © Lydia Kruger/Shutterstock, 26; © Gordon Swanson/Shutterstock, 16, 17, 22 (inset).

While every care has been taken to trace and acknowledge copyright, the publisher tenders their apologies for any accidental infringement where copyright has proved untraceable. Where the attempt has been unsuccessful, the publisher welcomes information that would redress the situation.

1 3 5 6 4 2

Contents

Glossary words
When a word is printed in **bold**, you can look up its meaning in the Glossary on page 31.

Families

Families live in countries all around the world. Some of your friends may have a family just like yours. Some of your friends may have families very different from yours.

This family has a grandfather, a mother, and a daughter.

Families are made up of different people, young and old. All people in a family are called family members.

This family has five family members.

Parents and Children

There are parents and children in most families. The parents look after the children and give them the things they need.

A mother likes to make sure her children eat well.

Many families have two parents, but some have one parent. A family may have many children or just one.

This family has a daughter and a mother.

Mothers and Fathers

Parents are the mothers or the fathers of their children. Many different people are parents or take the **role** of parents.

This man and boy are father and son.

Brothers and Sisters

The children in a family are brother or sister to each other. Brothers and sisters are also called siblings. To their parents, children are sons or daughters.

These two boys are siblings, or brothers.

Family Connections

Family members are connected in many different ways. They are connected by birth, **adoption**, **foster care** relationships, or marriage.

The people who make up a family are connected to each other.

When a mother has a baby, the baby is related to her by blood. The baby is also related to the father and to any brothers and sisters.

This man and woman are the parents of their baby.

Adoptive Families

Sometimes children who are not able to live with their **birth parents** are adopted by a family. Adoptive parents become the children's father and mother.

This girl was adopted by a family with two boys.

Foster Families

Families who look after children whose parents cannot care for them are called foster families. Foster children live with their foster families for as long as they need the care.

Children who grow up in a foster family together take on the roles of siblings.

Stepfamilies

Children whose parents marry a second time have stepfamilies. These children belong to two families. The stepfamily is the family of their new parent.

Children get to know new members of their family by spending time with them.

A stepparent is a new mother or father who comes into a family through marriage. This can happen if a father or mother dies, or if the parents **divorce**.

This mother and daughter make a stepfamily with the father and son.

15

Stepbrothers and Stepsisters

Two families with children sometimes join to make a new family. The children of each family are stepsisters and stepbrothers to each other.

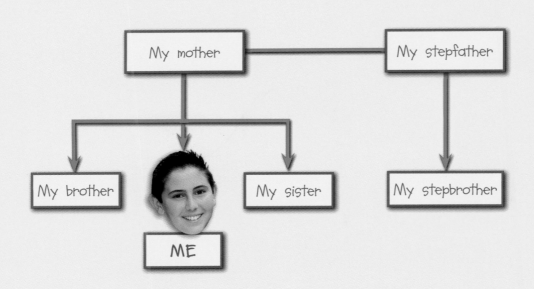

My mother — My stepfather

My brother   ME   My sister   My stepbrother

The child of my stepfather is my stepbrother.

Half-brothers and Half-sisters

Half-brothers and half-sisters are children who share one birth parent. They may have the same mother but different fathers.

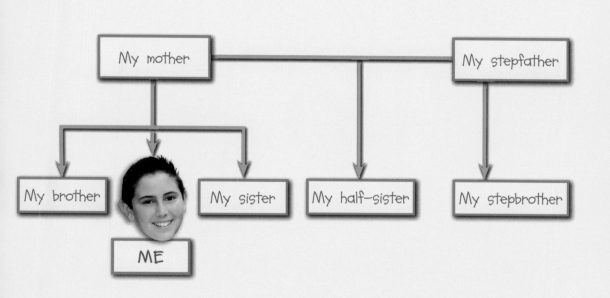

The child of my mother and my stepfather is my half-sister.

Grandparents

Grandparents are an important part of families. They are the parents of the children's parents. Some grandparents live with a family and help look after the children.

Grandparents often have plenty of time to spend with their grandchildren.

Sometimes, a parent dies or cannot look after their children properly. Grandparents may take on the role of parents.

This grandmother has a close relationship with her grandchild.

The Extended Family

Parents and siblings are often the most important family members to young children. There are some other important people in families, too. They are part of the **extended family**.

An extended family includes aunts, uncles, and cousins.

Great-grandparents

Some children have great-grandparents.
A great-grandparent is the father or mother
of a grandparent.

A great-grandparent
is often the oldest
member of the
extended family.

Aunts, Uncles, and Cousins

In many **cultures**, the brothers and sisters of the parents are called aunts and uncles. The children of the aunts and uncles are called cousins.

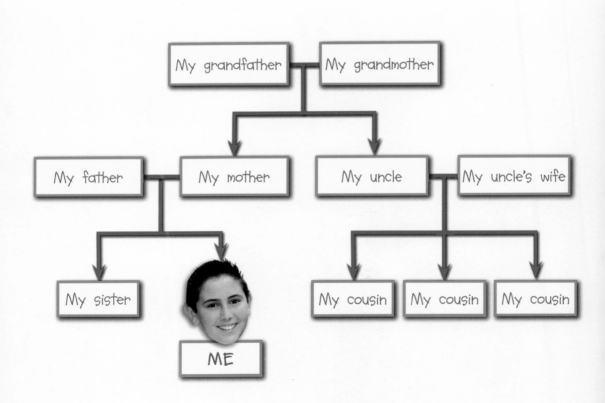

The children of my uncle and his wife are my cousins.

Some cultures use different names for different types of aunts and uncles. In Denmark, the mother's sister is called *moster* and the father's sister is called *faster*.

In Denmark, an aunt is called a *moster*.

Chinese Families

In China, the children of a mother's sister sometimes call each other "brother" or "sister." The children of the father's brother might do so as well.

The children in some Chinese families may call each other "brother" or "sister."

Indigenous Australian Family Groups

In some Indigenous Australian cultures, a mother's sisters are also mothers to her children. Her brothers are called uncles. A father's brothers are also called the fathers of his children.

Some Indigenous Australian children live in extended families.

Relations by Marriage

Most families have relations by marriage. When a husband and wife marry, the members of their families become connected by marriage.

This wedding in Africa celebrates two families joining together.

In some cultures, people who are related by marriage are called in-laws. Your brother's wife is called your sister-in-law.

husband

wife

father-in-law

mother-in-law

The parents of the wife are the in-laws of the husband.

A Family Tree

A family tree shows the connections between people in an extended family. Different **generations** are usually shown on different levels.

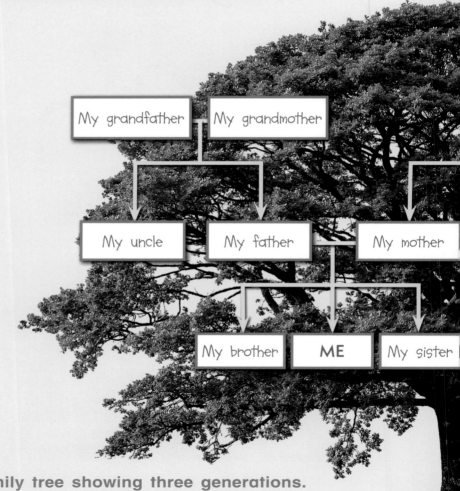

This is a family tree showing three generations.

Every person in a family has a position on the family tree diagram.

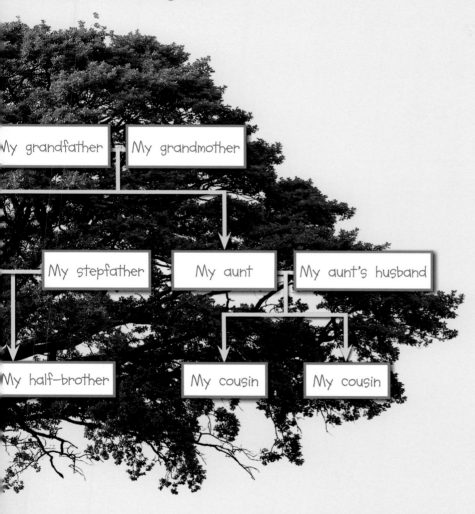

My grandfather   My grandmother

My stepfather   My aunt   My aunt's husband

My half-brother   My cousin   My cousin

Your Family Tree

The names of the people in a family can be joined together on a family tree.

Try this!

Draw your family tree. Keep it simple by showing only the closest members of your family.

My Family Tree

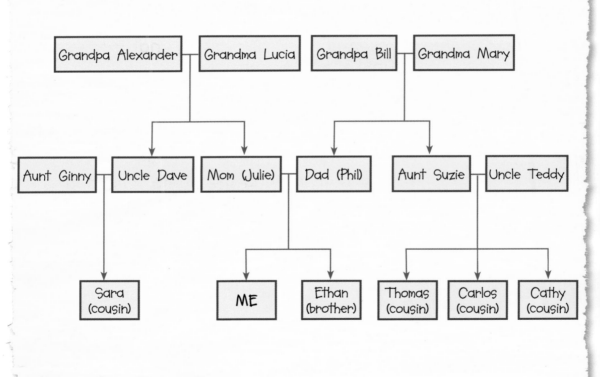

Glossary

adoption   when a child becomes part of the family by legal means

birth parents   parents who are related to the child by blood

cultures   groups of people with the same traditions and practices

divorce   legally end a marriage

extended family   all the members of a family, not just the parents and children

foster care   to raise a child who is not related to the family by birth or adoption

generations   the groups of people in a family who are usually born around the same time and are on the same level in a family tree

role   the position or part that a person plays in life

Index